W9-BGM-661

3/05

First Facts™

Community Helpers at Work

A Day in the Life of a
Garbage Collector

by Nate LeBoutillier

Consultant:
Steve Ridzon
Technical Programs Coordinator
Solid Waste Association of North America
Silver Spring, Maryland

Capstone
press

Mankato, Minnesota

First Facts is published by Capstone Press
151 Good Counsel Drive, P.O. Box 669, Mankato, Minnesota 56002
www.capstonepress.com

Library of Congress Cataloging-in-Publication Data
LeBoutillier, Nate.
  A day in the life of a garbage collector / by Nate LeBoutillier.
  p. cm.—(First facts. Community helpers at work)
  Includes bibliographical references and index.
  ISBN 0-7368-2629-7 (hardcover)
  1. Sanitation workers—Juvenile literature. 2. Refuse and refuse disposal—Juvenile literature
[1. Sanitation workers. 2. Occupations.] I. Title. II. Series.
HD8039.S257L4 2005
628.4'42'023—dc22   2003024651

Summary: This book follows a garbage collector through his day and describes his occupation
    and what his job requires of him.

Editorial Credits
Amanda Doering, editor; Jennifer Bergstrom, series designer; Molly Nei, book designer;
    Eric Kudalis, product planning editor

Photo Credits
All photos by Capstone Press/Gary Sundermeyer except page 20 (left), Atlantic Sales and Salvage
    and page 17, Creatas

Artistic Effects
Capstone Press/Gary Sundermeyer, 4, 6, 15, 19

Capstone Press would like to thank Rick Goff and Waste Management, Mankato, Minnesota, for
    their assistance in creating this book.

1 2 3 4 5 6 09 08 07 06 05 04

Table of Contents

When do garbage collectors start their days?

Garbage collectors wake up early in the morning. They start work when most people are still sleeping. Rick the garbage collector arrives at the office. He picks up his paperwork and swipes his **time card** to start the day.

Fun Fact!
There are about 100,000 garbage trucks in the United States.

4:30 in the morning

5

How important is safety to garbage collectors?

Safety is very important to garbage collectors. Once a week, Rick goes to safety meetings. At the meetings, he learns how to keep himself and others safe on the job.

5:00 in the
morning

7

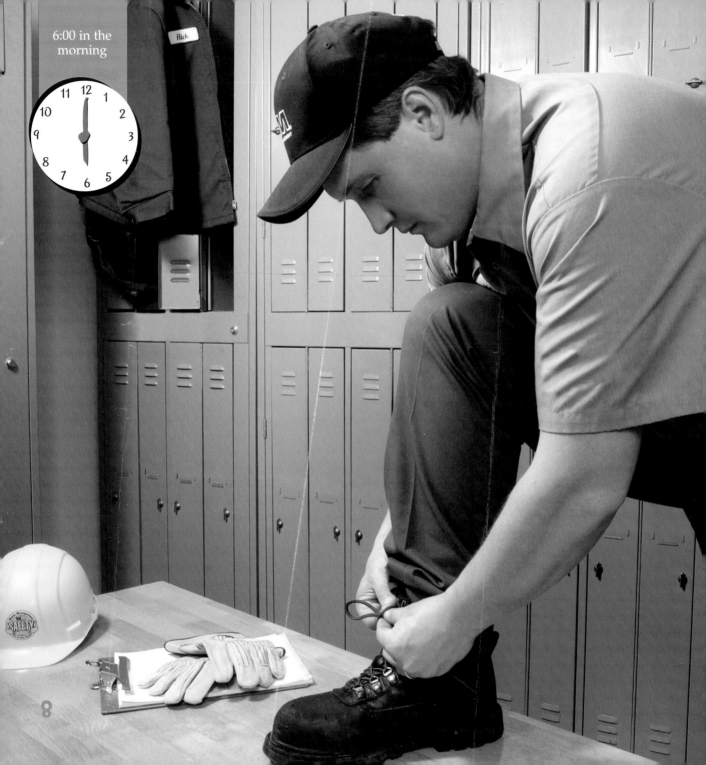

6:00 in the
morning

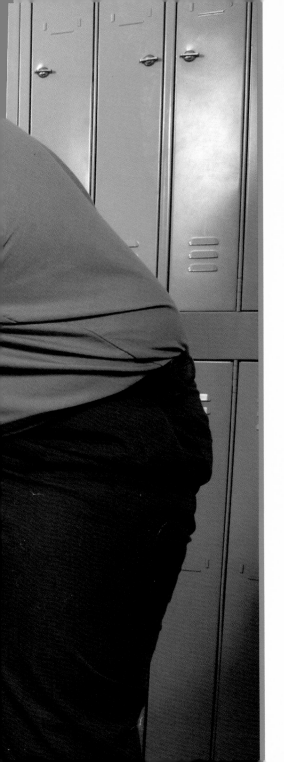

What do garbage collectors wear?

Garbage collectors wear shirts, pants, gloves, and steel-toed boots. Gloves keep Rick's hands safe from sharp objects, such as broken glass. Rick's boots keep his feet safe from falling garbage. Garbage collectors also wear hard hats when they dump garbage.

What do garbage collectors drive?

Garbage collectors drive trucks. The garbage truck has a large bin to hold trash. Rick checks the truck for problems each morning. This morning, he fills the tires with air.

Fun Fact!
Some garbage trucks have two sets of controls. Garbage collectors can drive from the right or left side of the truck.

WASTE MANAGEME

WASTE MANAGEMENT
(555) 442-1137

6:30 in the morning

11

What do garbage collectors do?

Garbage collectors drive different **routes** every day. They stop at houses and buildings to pick up garbage.

7:00 in the morning

A lift on Rick's truck picks up garbage cans. It dumps the garbage into the truck. The garbage is crushed to make room for more.

13

11:30 in the
morning

14

Who helps garbage collectors?

Mechanics help garbage collectors by taking care of the trucks. Mechanics fix trucks when they break down. Today, Jeremy checks a truck for problems.

People can also help garbage collectors. They can help by putting their garbage neatly into bags and cans.

What happens when the truck is full?

When the truck is full, it is time to dump the garbage. Rick dumps his truck at a holding area.

At some holding areas, the garbage is sorted. Some of the garbage is **recycled**. The rest of the garbage is taken to a **landfill**. At the landfill, the garbage will be covered with a layer of dirt.

17

2:00 in the afternoon

18

How do garbage collectors end their days?

Garbage collectors have work to do after the garbage is dumped. Rick puts fuel in his truck for tomorrow. He fills out paperwork in the office. Rick swipes his time card and goes home to rest for another day.

Amazing but True!

Garbage trucks can be painted any color. Some companies have rainbow-colored trucks. The most popular color for garbage trucks is white.

Shovel

Truck

Garbage can

Lift

Hard hat

Safety vest
Garbage collectors must wear brightly colored safety vests in the truck yard and on the route. People can easily see these bright vests.

Gloves

Recycle bin

21

Glossary

landfill (LAND-fil)—an area where garbage is buried; at a landfill, garbage is stacked and covered with dirt.

mechanic (muh-KAN-ik)—someone who operates or fixes machines

recycle (ree-SYE-kuhl)—to make new items from old items; cans, plastic, paper, and glass can be recycled.

route (ROUT)—a series of places a garbage collector visits to pick up garbage

time card (TIME KARD)—a card used to record the time a worker is on the job

Read More

Brill, Marlene Targ. *Garbage Trucks.* Pull Ahead Books. Minneapolis: Lerner, 2005.

Leeper, Angela. *The Landfill.* Field Trip! Chicago: Heinemann, 2004.

Internet Sites

FactHound offers a safe, fun way to find Internet sites related to this book. All of the sites on FactHound have been researched by our staff.

Here's how:
1. Visit *www.facthound.com*
2. Type in this special code **0736826297** for age-appropriate sites. Or enter a search word related to this book for a more general search.
3. Click on the **Fetch It** button.

FactHound will fetch the best sites for you!

Index

Sorrow's Journey

WORDS OF COMFORT TO HEAL THE GRIEVING HEART

BY

TWYLA FISHER

Frederick Fell Publishers, Inc.

2131 Hollywood Boulevard, Suite 305 Hollywood, Florida 33020

(954) 925-5242

e-mail: fellpub@aol.com

Visit our Web site at www.fellpub.com

Frederick Fell Publishers, Inc.
2131 Hollywood Boulevard, Suite 305
Hollywood, Florida 33020
(954) 925-5242
e-mail: fellpub@aol.com
Visit our Web site at www.fellpub.com

10 9 8 7 6 5 4 3 2 1

ISBN: 0-88391-046-2
Printed in China

I THOUGHT I COULD DESCRIBE A STATE, MAKE A MAP OF
SORROW. SORROW HOWEVER TURNS OUT TO BE NOT A
STATE BUT A PROCESS.

C.S. LEWIS, 1898-1963

INTRODUCTION

When the spouses of four of my good friends died in one year, I wanted to console them with something other than flowers. I searched for books to give but could find none that appealed to me. I wanted to give my friends a book that helped with the grieving process, in addition to providing comforting insights and a reminder of the beauty of life, even at times of great grief. Because I felt there was a need for this support, I decided to write *Sorrow's Journey: Words of Comfort to Heal the Grieving Heart.* I have written it as a road map through the very human journey of grief. The book is designed so a person can pick it up and read from any page, not necessarily from beginning to end.

It is my hope that the experiences, quotations, and beautiful images included here will serve as a source of guidance and healing.

Blessings on your journey.
Twyla Fisher

BLESSED ARE THOSE WHO GRIEVE, FOR THEY WILL BE COMFORTED.

MATTHEW 5:4

HAVE PATIENCE WITH ALL THINGS,
BUT FIRST OF ALL WITH YOURSELF.
ST. FRANCIS DE SALES,
1567-1622

Knowing what to expect on the grief journey can help us through this difficult time and remind us that this path has a beginning, middle, and end. We have a destination — to find peace of mind so our lives begin to feel familiar to us again.

Included in this book is an explanation of the grieving process as well as personal experiences on how others have worked through their pain. They are —

- Meaningful rituals

- Sharing our feelings/opening our hearts to others

- Facing our grief; tears are natural and healing and help bring resolution to our loss

- Facing fear and loneliness

- Handling anger and frustration

- The need for proper rest, nutrition, and exercise (be kind to yourself)

- Spending time with Mother Nature

- Forgiveness — journal/ letter writing

- Tips on handling holidays and other special occasions

- Simple pleasures to relieve tension and loneliness

- Community and national grief

- Faith/meditation

- Hope for the future

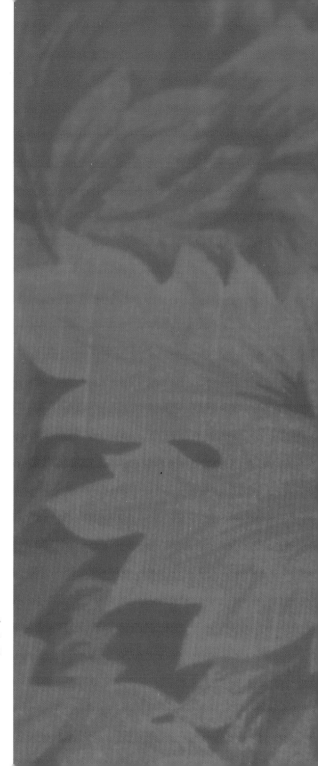

Look well into thyself; there is a source of strength which will always spring up if thou wilt always look there.

Marcus Aurelius, 121-180 A.D.

Absolute calm is not the law of the ocean. And it is the same with the ocean of life.

Mohandas Gandhi, 1869-1948

*S*ooner or later in life each of us will experience overwhelming grief from the death of someone we love. We shared love, unforgettable experiences, joys, and sorrows. Now we feel empty, alone, and in pain. It is human nature to want to hold on to those we love, to cling to the past and the familiar, and to resist facing the unknown. Yet, to quote Helen Keller, "What we once enjoyed and deeply loved we can never lose, for all that we love deeply becomes part of us."

With the initial shock from the death of a loved one, we often just feel numb. Sometimes this is a blessing, helping us through the first painful hours and days. However, as the numbness begins to wear away, we may be left with confusing emotions and questions. We ask, "Why did this happen? Where is my loved one now? Who am I now? What am I supposed to learn?" Facing our loss can often launch us into a search for answers to life's most perplexing questions. In her book, *After the Darkest Hour*, Kathleen Brehony, Ph.D., says, "It is change and loss that create suffering, and it is suffering that propels us from the quiet shores of everyday life into the turbulent sea in which real growth occurs. Considering the emotional costs of the journey, we must take comfort in the assurance that a conscious life is golden."

Funerals, memorial services, and other meaningful rituals help us face the reality of loss and begin the process of grieving. We do not always have to follow tradition, however.

Death is a challenge. It tells us not to waste time...it tells us to tell each other right now that we love one another.

Leo F. Buscaglia, 1924-1998

*J*oe's father died suddenly on New Year's Day several years ago. The family was in shock, they had just spent a happy holiday together and suddenly found themselves in the midst of grieving. Because Joe's mom was in poor health, she asked him to be responsible for the memorial service.

Give Sorrow Words

WILLIAM SHAKESPEARE, 1564-1616

The day before the service Joe asked family members and friends for a personal contribution to honor the memory of his dad. Each went into a room alone to privately audio tape their thoughts and feelings. Because they had time to reflect, family members found it easier to share deeply. The next day at the service, after traditional prayers, inspirational readings, and beautiful background music, the tapes were played on the loud speaker. Joe's dad was a kind, loving, and hardworking man and the personal emotions of the audio remembrances reminded everyone in attendance of those special traits.

Joe's eight-year-old daughter Jannea shared on the tape, "I knew Grandpa loved me because he always seemed so glad to see me." Tears filled the mourners' eyes as they listened to the innocent expression of love for a beloved grandfather, now gone. It was that sort of personal experience that made this unorthodox part of the service so meaningful.

A year or so later, Jannea heard the music "Pachebel Canon." Her face lit up as she said, "That's the song they played at Grandpa's funeral. Every time I hear it I think of him." Personalized observances warm our hearts and create lasting memories.

An unusual service for saying "goodbye" to her husband was held by a friend of mine. They lived near foothills where her husband liked to hike. My friend, her children, and their families decided to a have a special picnic in the mountains celebrating their husband and father's life. His picture as well as a special place setting for him at the picnic table were their focus. My friend said she felt her husband's presence with them as they ate their lunch and were reminded of the many happy occasions they had all shared. After the picnic their loved one's ashes were buried under a beautiful old tree as each said his or her "goodbye."

Special ceremonies with family and friends such as planting a tree, flowers, or the dedication of a park bench are also wonderful tributes honoring the memories of the people we love. Since relationships differ, it is important to do whatever feels most meaningful to you.

After the funeral or memorial service we need to continue talking with concerned family and friends about our sorrow. Choose wisely, however. It's important to find friends who encourage us to move through the grieving process in our own way and at our own pace. People may offer comfort by saying, "Time will heal." Time does heal, that's true. But it heals only if we have faced our loss. Many people want to be helpful but don't know what to do. Speak your truth. If you are the person grieving, let others know how they can best minister to you. You will be doing them and yourself a favor.

The journey of grief often allows us to feel compassion and empathy for the needs and pains of others. Abraham Lincoln said, "To ease another's heartache is to forget one's own."

CLIMB THE MOUNTAINS AND GET THEIR GOOD TIDINGS. NATURE'S PEACE WILL FLOW INTO YOU AS SUNSHINE FLOWS INTO TREES.

JOHN MUIR, 1838-1914

WHEN I HEARD THE CHURCH BELLS RING, I THOUGHT I HEARD THE VOICE OF GOD.
ALBERT SCHWEITZER, 1875-1965

One inspiring story of compassion and generosity is that of Reg and Maggie Green, whose son, seven-year-old Nicholas, was killed by highway robbers while his family was vacationing in Italy. In the midst of their pain, both Reg and Maggie were concerned with saving other lives and decided to donate Nicholas' organs to seven seriously ill Italians. The people of Italy were so moved by the Green's kindness that there has been an increase in organ donations of nearly thirty percent. Reg and Maggie have since produced a video and Reg has authored a book, both entitled *The Nicholas Effect*, which have also increased organ donations worldwide. Such is the Green's example. The gift of life, given even at the moment of death, helps to heal the wounds of loss.

In memory of Nicholas, the Green's, who live in Bodega Bay, California, had an 18-foot bell monument constructed and dedicated to children worldwide. It was placed in a beautiful meadow with a distant view of the ocean near the pre-school that Nicholas had attended. From the pyramid structure hang 130 bells of all shapes and sizes donated by Italians. The largest bronze bell is inscribed with the names of Nicholas and those receiving his donated organs. It was blessed by Pope John Paul II in Rome. Bells are an important part of the Italian culture and every village has a bell tower which tolls for births, marriages, and funerals.

Reg and Maggie have received hundreds of letters and cards of condolence. Many parents have mentioned that they now spend more quality time with their children, which the Greens hope will be yet another positive result of their tragedy. For the Greens, the joy of life continues as they nurture Nicholas' siblings.

The story of Nicholas, whom family and friends recall as a loving, amazingly mature seven-year-old, has touched the lives of people worldwide. In their grief, his parents have created a healing legacy that insures that Nicholas will always be remembered.

THE SUNLIGHT OF GRACE IS ALL AROUND YOU. BUT YOU MUST OPEN THE WINDOW OF YOUR HEART TO GET THE BENEFIT OF THE SUNLIGHT.

SAI BABA, 1926-

Switzerland and had been college roommates. We could not understand how the life of this beautiful and talented person could be suddenly ended at such a young age. This is something we all question when death comes unexpectedly to the young. There are no easy answers. We can only speculate that perhaps our loved ones have completed their journeys here on Earth and have moved on.

After Jan's funeral, her friends spontaneously decided to go out to lunch in her honor. They found that sharing tears and laughter over stories about their friend gave them some solace as well as renewed heart connections with each other. Memories are a blessing that help us work through the pain.

Over the years, several of Jan's friends have maintained a warm

Memories shared with caring friends and relatives are a healthy way of dealing with loss. When my daughter, Cynthia, was in her twenties, one of her friends, Jan, was killed in the crash of a small plane. Cynthia was devastated — she had lost a wonderful friend. The girls had spent a summer together in

friendship with Jan's mother, which has been a continued source of comfort and joy for everyone.

Remember that grief is a journey — a journey with a destination of adjustment, inner peace and, finally, wholeness. This trip can only be made by the mourner, traveling the road step-by-step. Each grief journey is unique and cannot be compared to others. Yet each person's experience of this journey has lessons for us all. The telling of stories helps others to see they are not alone.

GOD GAVE US MEMORIES THAT WE MIGHT HAVE ROSES IN DECEMBER.
SIR JAMES M. BARRIE, 1860-1937

GO OUTSIDE, TO THE FIELDS,
ENJOY NATURE AND THE
SUNSHINE, GO OUT AND TRY
TO RECAPTURE HAPPINESS IN
YOURSELF AND IN GOD.

ANNE FRANK, 1929-1945

When my father became ill on his 70th birthday and it was apparent that his condition was serious, I was called to Nebraska. He lived a few days after my arrival and I was with him at the time of his death.

After the funeral, I could stay with my mother for only a short time since I had to go back to my job in California. I was extremely sad about leaving, but felt fine once I got home. Returning for a visit the following summer, however, I immediately felt an overwhelming sadness and knew it was because I was missing Dad. It finally occurred to me that I hadn't finished grieving and had suppressed feelings of sadness for almost a year. It would have been much easier for me — and my family — had I dealt with my grief at the time of my father's death.

Western culture often teaches us to retreat from the task of grieving, which simply tends to postpone and prolong the pain. Although we resist expressing emotions for fear of losing control, we need to accept our feelings and give ourselves permission to be sad. Grief faced helps to bring resolution to our loss. "Let mourning stop when one's grief is fully expressed," said Confucius.

My mother died ten years after my father's death. She had been in poor health for many years and, when her condition became critical, I returned to Nebraska on the evening before she died. Although she appeared to be unconscious, I sensed she knew I was with her. After spending several hours at her bedside, I went to a nearby waiting room to rest a bit. Shortly after falling asleep, a nurse woke me to tell me that Mother had just died. I had hoped to be with her at the exact time of her death just as I had been with Dad. In my pain and confusion, I felt guilty for taking a nap instead of being with her, and I carried that guilt for several years. I have since learned that experts believe people often die shortly after loved ones leave the room. Oh, the unnecessary guilt we place on ourselves. It is some comfort to know that perhaps our loved ones had their own way of saying good bye to us and did not feel that we had neglected them.

In the years after Dad's death, I saw my mother once or twice a year. Because of her poor health, each time we parted I felt I might never see her again. I mourned a bit after each "goodbye" and when Mother died I had already worked through some of the pain of losing her.

Since grief is an intense response to the loss of someone we deeply loved and to the ending of a treasured relationship, we mourn in order to adjust to the pain of separation. However, we do not always mourn in the same way, especially when a loved one has been ill for a long time. No two griefs or relationships are the same, even within one family.

After the death of a loved one, we may experience a variety of emotions, including fear and loneliness, as well as overwhelming sadness. We need to accept those feelings as normal and be patient with ourselves. Crying releases feelings of sadness and despair. Unfortunately, we have often been conditioned to suppress tears. Well-meaning friends and relatives may tell us it is time to "quit crying," but they may not fully understand the grieving process. Tears are natural and healthy; this is the time for them to flow freely. Our tears may also help others release pain, as sharing tears can be healing.

WE DO NOT REMEMBER DAYS, WE REMEMBER MOMENTS.
CESARE PAVESE, 1908-1950

Have courage for the great sorrows of life and patience for the small ones, and when you have laboriously accomplished your daily task, go to sleep in peace. God is awake.

Victor Hugo, 1802-1885

HE WHO LACKS TIME TO
MOURN, LACKS TIME TO MEND.
WILLIAM SHAKESPEARE,
(1564-1616)

When Bob, an old friend, told me that he wept in remembrance of his wife for at least two years after her death, I was reminded of a quote by Washington Irving: "There is a sacredness in tears. They are not the mark of weakness, but of power. They speak more eloquently than ten thousand tongues. They are messengers of overwhelming grief, of deep contrition, and of unspeakable love."

Part of our grief is often fear of the unknown, of not being able to make it by ourselves. Or it may involve fear of our own mortality. Fear is an emotion that needs to be addressed — not suppressed or dismissed as irrational. It is, after all, a natural reaction to love lost.

Occassionally mourners feel the need to blame someone for the seeming-injustice of their loss. We may find ourselves angry at the person who has died because of the unfulfilled hopes and dreams their death has destroyed. Frustration and shortness of temper are typical feelings experienced by many in the throes of grief. If you have those feelings, know that you are not alone and what you are feeling is normal.

Loneliness is another painful aspect of the grief journey. Yet, many people find they develop an appreciation for time alone and discover the value, and even the pleasure, of introspection and reflection that solitude can bring. Quiet time for feeding our spirit through reading, prayer, and meditation contributes to inner peace and healing.

I ONLY WENT OUT FOR A WALK, AND FINALLY
CONCLUDED TO STAY OUT TILL SUNDOWN, FOR
GOING OUT, I FOUND, WAS REALLY GOING IN.

JOHN MUIR, 1838-1914

Sleep habits are often disrupted during the grieving process. Some people find it difficult to sleep and get up each morning feeling mentally and physically fatigued while others sleep more than ever. Taking time for proper rest, nutritious meals, and physical exercise will help provide needed strength. Gently let go of unnecessary tasks and responsibilities which drain life energy that you need to complete the grieving process. It is important to be kind to yourself during this stressful time.

Exercise, especially in the sunlight, stimulates natural chemicals in our brains that make us less prone to depression. Step outside each day, even if just for a few minutes. Walking is a wonderful way to clear our thinking, release pent-up emotions, and help us sleep better. There is an ancient Roman saying: "Solvitur ambulando." Translated it means, "It is solved by walking."

A few years ago when Carolyn, a long time friend, was having difficulty adjusting to the death of her husband, I invited her to visit me in California. Carolyn had always enjoyed vacationing in the San Francisco area but was reluctant because of memories she had of former trips to the Bay Area with her husband.

Knowing her love of the outdoors, I arranged for most of our days to be spent on nature outings. We walked across the Golden Gate Bridge, took a boat ride on San Francisco Bay, and hiked on beaches and in State parks. Absorbing the beauty of the ocean and landscape and breathing fresh air seemed to comfort my friend. It was great for me, too. Spending time in nature helps heal our spirits.

KEEP THE GREEN TREE IN YOUR
HEART AND PERHAPS THE SINGING
BIRD WILL COME.

CHINESE PROVERB

*D*ebra and her brothers and sister had an exceptionally close and loving relationship with their mother, who died quite unexpectedly. Though Debra had been a Hospice worker for several years, she found she was unprepared for the pain she was experiencing. She says she felt as if she were looking across a lake and couldn't see the opposite shore because the fog of grief was so thick. As the months passed, Debra spent more time out-of-doors and finally began to recover from the overwhelming pain. She thinks Mother Nature seems to be healing her. Debra recently said, "I hear the birds singing again, feel the wind and the sun on my face, enjoy the colors, and appreciate nature's beauty more than I ever have. I feel my mother's presence in the beauty of nature."

And what of unresolved conflicts and pain? Keeping a journal or writing an imaginary letter to someone who has died can help. Expressing our full range of feelings — love and appreciation, as well as anger, resentment, and frustration — helps us heal. We can conclude our letters with a statement of forgiveness of ourselves and our loved ones for any previous words or deeds. Forgiveness is a giant step towards healing. We can even read the letter out loud, perhaps placing a photo of our loved one in front of us. This ritual can be completed by burning the letter, symbolizing the release of attachment. Writing a letter from the heart and actually saying good-bye are steps of closure on the healing path.

Forgiveness is the fragrance the violet sheds on the heel that has crushed it.

Mark Twain, 1835-1910

Holidays can be some of the most painful days for mourners. By their very nature those special times are stressful and the added burden of grief makes them that much more difficult. Increased sadness on holidays can be expected and is best handled by preparing ahead and facing one day at a time.

When Betty, a dear friend, lost her husband of many years just before Thanksgiving, she dreaded the holidays. She and her daughters finally decided to change their traditional customs at least for that year. Altering traditions helped them get through those difficult days fairly well. Trying to continue with our usual ways can be both physically and emotionally exhausting.

You might wish to forego activities such as putting up holiday decorations and, instead, use flowers or candles to brighten your home. If sending holiday greetings, the inclusion of a brief memorial of your loved one's life can be a fitting tribute.

Feelings of sadness may be triggered at any time by memories of past holidays, anniversaries, or even hearing special songs. Though mourning doesn't go on forever, there will be times when you will have memories that evoke deep emotion.

To everything there is a season, and a time to every purpose under heaven.

ECCLESIASTES, 3:1

Although we no longer live near each other, Betty and I occasionally spend time together. On the first anniversary of her husband's death, she happened to be visiting me. I was grateful she wasn't alone that day and, also, that she felt free to shed healing tears. We can allow ourselves permission to cry, feel our sadness and, at the same time, appreciate moments of pleasure in our lives.

Simple pleasures in life provide meaning and relieve tension. Listen to inspiring music; enroll in a class; take a little journey; share lunch with a friend; see an uplifting or funny movie. Laughter provides moments of joy and releases wonderfully healing endorphins. Joy is a possibility for our lives, maybe not for a while, but eventually when grief is resolved and we begin to see the light at the end of the tunnel.

A WORLD OF GRIEF AND PAIN,
FLOWERS BLOOM EVEN THEN.

KOBAYASHI ISSA, 1763-1827

On September 11, 2001, our nation experienced shock, outrage, and fear. For many, it brought back memories of the dark days lived through other wars. We all have to face the deaths of loved ones; we expect that. But witnessing sudden, senseless loss of life and suffering caused by hate is difficult for most to comprehend.

When speaking about death in his book *When Bad Things Happen to Good People*, Rabbi Harold Kushner said, "We can't explain it any more than we can explain life itself. We can't control it, or sometimes even postpone it. All we can do is try to rise beyond the question 'why did it happen?' and begin to ask the question 'what do I do now that it has happened?'"

After the attacks there was an immediate outpouring of support, not only in the U.S. but throughout the world. There were candlelight vigils and prayer services throughout the land as the singing of "God Bless America" inspired us. For days, lines of people waited patiently all over America to donate blood.

AS ONE SMALL CANDLE MAY LIGHT A THOUSAND, SO
THE LIGHT HERE KINDLED HATH SHONE UNTO MANY,
YEA, IN SOME SORT TO OUR WHOLE NATION.

WILLIAM BRADFORD, 1590-1657

Clergy of all faiths and politicians shared words of encouragement.
They stressed the importance of not hating the Muslim population for
what a few had done. We were reminded that Islam teaches love, not
hate.

People helped where they could. Chefs from the best New York
restaurants (using three boats anchored close to the scene of the attack
in lower Manhattan) worked together to provide thousands of meals for
brave firefighters, police, and rescue workers. The chefs and their helpers
were referred to as "chefs with spirit." This was done in the same spirit
as when we, as caring friends and neighbors, take a homemade meal to
families who are mourning. We humans are resilient and often bond after
tragedy.

was reminded of the spirit of giving during World War II when I lived in North Platte, Nebraska, a Union Pacific Railroad center located in the heart of farmland. On December 17, 1941, shortly after Pearl Harbor, a large group of relatives and friends of the men of Nebraska's 134th Infantry gathered in the railroad depot with food and coffee, waiting for the train carrying the soldiers, which was supposed to go through North Platte on its way to an unknown destination. After meeting several trains, the greeters finally realized their boys weren't coming through North Platte so they showered the last train of the day, containing troops from Kansas, with their goodies. The appreciation and joy of the soldiers touched the hearts of the greeters and that was the birth of the North Platte Canteen.

The women of North Platte and surrounding towns and farms provided free homemade sandwiches, cookies, cakes, and coffee for over six million servicemen and women. They met every troop train coming through their town for the next five years. As a young girl, I was a witness to the gift of community from my mother and other women of that rural area of Nebraska. Perhaps today's children will learn about unity and collective strength from us.

It is one of the most beautiful compensations of life that no man can sincerely try to help another without helping himself.

Ralph Waldo Emerson, 1803-1882

We join together when experiencing community and national grief. The Vietnam Wall and the Oklahoma City Memorial, visited by millions of people each year, are national symbols of healing. Another example of community healing is the AIDS quilt.

Dr. Susan Farrell, a psychologist in northern California, states that "participation in community events or projects helps mourners feel less alone and isolated in their grief, allowing us to pool our psychological and spiritual strengths and borrow coping skills from each other. Some group projects

or events allow us to commemorate and celebrate the lives of lost loved ones. When my brother died of AIDS, I found it immeasurably healing to design and sew a panel to be added to the AIDS quilt, reflecting upon his life and gaining more perspective on his absence in my own life as I sewed."

Healing our sorrow takes inner strength and patience. We can, however, begin to overcome our grief with the support of family and friends, through participation in symbolic memorials, and from the outpouring of caring by complete strangers.

FAITH IS THE BIRD THAT SINGS WHEN DAWN
IS STILL DARK.

RABINDRANATH TAGORE, 1861-1941

SOLITUDE IS NOT SOMETHING YOU MUST HOPE FOR IN THE FUTURE. RATHER, IT IS A DEEPENING OF THE PRESENT.

THOMAS MERTON, 1915-1968

Having faith, which is trust in the future and a belief in something greater than oneself, also helps us heal. It is knowing that God will support us and give us the needed strength to face life's challenges and be at peace. Faith does not necessarily mean we have to belong to a specific religion. However, if you belong to a church or a prayer or meditation group, this is not the time to abandon that security. Continuing a familiar practice with friends of like mind can be comforting.

WHERE THERE IS PEACE IN MEDITATION, THERE IS NEITHER ANXIETY NOR DOUBT.

ST. FRANCIS OF ASSISI, 1181-1226

When in the midst of grief we tend to relive our sorrows over and over in our minds, increasing the pain in our hearts. Paramahansa Yogananda, a wise Indian who came to America as a delegate to an international religious convention in 1920 and remained a spiritual teacher in the United States for more than 30 years, advised, "When the thorn of misery is piercing your heart, take it out with the thorn of meditation." Meditation is a practical and proven method for lifting the mind above the worries and pressures of life. It is a journey into one's soul.

Among the many methods of meditation, I believe the following is one of the most effective as well as easiest to learn. These suggestions are basic guidelines, however, and can be adapted to your individual needs. Don't get discouraged if you have trouble concentrating at first — everyone does. Be patient with yourself.

LEARN TO GET IN TOUCH WITH THE SILENCE
WITHIN YOURSELF AND KNOW THAT EVERYTHING
IN THIS LIFE HAS A PURPOSE.
ELISABETH KUBLER-ROSS, 1926-

1. Find a quiet place where you can be alone with no interruptions, having the attitude that there is nothing else that must be done during your quiet time. It's helpful to have a regular meditation time so it becomes part of your daily routine.

2. Make yourself as comfortable as possible — loosen any tight clothing; take off your shoes. If the body is comfortable, the mind will be less distracted.

3. Sit in a straight-backed chair. Westerners usually find sitting in a chair more comfortable than sitting on the floor in the lotus posture, which is practiced in the East. Your spine should be straight but relaxed, with your feet flat on the floor to keep the blood circulating properly. Position a firm pillow at your back, if necessary.

4. Place your hands in your lap any way they are comfortable. Many people keep the palms up, indicating a receptive mode.

5. Scan your body for tension. If you notice tension or soreness in your neck, gently roll your head clockwise and then counter clockwise a few times. If your shoulders feel tense, shrug and release them. Tense and relax any other parts of the body that feel tight or sore. Take a few deep breaths and tell your body to "relax and let go."

6. Focus your attention on your heart area and your breathing. There is a direct link between our breathing habits and the restlessness of the mind. When the breath becomes calm, so does the mind.

7. Try to be centered in the here and now. We all have the habit of reliving the past and planning for the future. As thoughts arise, gently let them go and bring your attention back to the present.

8. Light a candle in front of you, concentrating on the flame for several minutes to help still the mind. Once you begin to relax, lightly close your eyes and visualize the flame between your eyebrows. After a few minutes, imagine the light flowing to your heart, bathing every feeling and emotion. If your mind begins to wander (and it will), bring your attention back to the heart area, releasing all worries and concerns. Continue meditating for as long as you feel focused and calm, but don't meditate for more than 15 to 20 minutes at first. Gently open your eyes and slowly focus on the world around you, closing your meditation with a peaceful heart.

Never give up hope that someday the pain will decrease and life will once again have meaning. Traditionally, the rainbow is a symbol of hope. Hanging a crystal in a sunlit window reflects rays of the rainbow and can be a beautiful reminder that there is hope. "Hope is like the sun, which, as we journey toward it, casts the shadow of our burden behind us." (Samuel Smiles, 1812-1904)

THE SOUL WOULD HAVE NO RAINBOW, HAD THE EYES NO TEARS.

JOHN VANCE CHENEY, 1848-1922

WHAT A CATERPILLAR CALLS THE END OF THE
WORLD THE MASTER CALLS A BUTTERFLY.

RICHARD BACH, 1936-

As we travel through the stages of grief, we ultimately gain strength and inner peace. We learn to appreciate and treasure time spent with our loved ones and honor their memory when we move on towards a full and happy life. The highest tribute we can pay them is to continue on the journey as fully and joyfully as possible and prepare for our own transition into the life beyond.

I will always be grateful to family members and friends who have so willingly shared their experiences of the grieving process with me. Thank you Alberta, Joe, Reg, Maggie, Bob, Carolyn, Debra, Betty and Susan. Allowing me to use your experiences as examples of overcoming the immense pain of your grief has made it possible to help others understand the steps and normal feelings we all go through when faced with the death of a loved one.

Thanks also to Hal Zina Bennett, Richard Scott, and my daughters, Pam and Cynthia, for your helpful suggestions and editing.

A warm and heartfelt thank you to you all.

Acknowledgments

Aurelius, Marcus (121-180 A.D.) Roman emperor.

Bach, Richard (1936-) American writer best know for his book *Jonathan Livingston Seagull.*

Barrie, Sir James M. (1860-1937) British author and playwright.

Bradford, William (1590-1657) Governor of Massachusetts; came to America on the Mayflower.

Buscaglia, Leo (1924-1998) American teacher, lecturer, and author on love.

Camus, Albert (1913-1960) French philosopher, author, and playwright. Nobel prize, 1957.

Cheney, John Vance (1848-1922) American author, poet, and librarian.

Confucius (551-479 B.C.) Chinese philospher and educator.

Emerson, Ralph Waldo (1803-1882) American poet, essayist, and philosopher.

Frank, Anne (1929-1945) Dutch-Jewish diarist; victim of the Holocaust.

Gandhi, Mohandas (1869-1948) Indian spiritual and political leader; advocate of non-violence.

Hugo, Victor (1802-1885) French novelist, poet, and playwright.

Irving, Washington (1783-1859) American writer, author of *The Legend of Sleepy Hollow.*

Issa, Kobayshi (1763-1827) Japanese poet, Haiku master.

Keller, Helen (1880-1968) American author and lecturer.

Kubler-Ross, Elisabeth (1926-) Swiss-born, U.S. psychiatrist, lecturer, and author. Known for her work on death and dying.

Lewis, C.S. (1898-1963) Irish author, Oxford professor.

Lincoln, Abraham (1809-1865) 16th U.S. President during Civil War.

Merton, Thomas (1915-1968) French-born American monk and author.

Muir, John (1838-1914) Scottish-born American naturalist.

Pavese, Cesare (1908-1950) Italian novelist, poet, and translator.

Sai Baba (1926-) Indian holy man and teacher.

St. Francis of Assisi (1181-1226) Italian founder of the Franciscan order of monks.

St. Francis de Sales (1567-1622) 16th century Bishop of Geneva.

Schweitzer, Albert (1875-1965) Alsatian/German theologian, philosopher, and mission doctor. Nobel prize, 1952.

Shakespeare, William (1564-1616) English playwright and poet.

Smiles, Samuel (1812-1904) Scottish reformer and author. Best known for his book *Self Help*.

Tagore, Rabindranath (1861-1941) Bengali poet, writer, composer, and painter. Nobel prize, 1913.

Twain, Mark (1835-1910) Pen name for Samuel L. Clemens. American humorist, writer, and lecturer.

In the midst of winter,
I found at last there
was within myself an
invincible summer.

ALBERT CAMUS,
1913-1960